Online Dating

Advice to Maximize Your Relationship Success on the Internet

Amy Evans

© 2016 Amy Evans

All rights reserved. This book or any portion thereof may not be reproduced or used in any manner whatsoever without the express written permission of the publisher except for the use of brief quotations in a book review.

Table of Contents

Introduction

Chapter 1 – How to Put Yourself out There to Attract Your Match

Chapter 2 – How to Pick the Right Match

Chapter 3 – How to Move On and Arrange a Meet-Up

Chapter 4 – Best Places to Meet-Up

Conclusion

Introduction

Modern life has added new ways to find the love of your life. Old mechanisms, like families arranging potential matches or meeting your partner at dances and parties, are out of date and have left many struggling to find love. Our lives are so busy with work and our social commitments that we often don't know where or when to meet new people. Online dating allows us to potentially meet millions of people, all from the comfort of our home.

Whether you are fed up going to busy clubs just so you can meet new people or whether you have other things to do in your free time, you should consider online dating. All you need is a stable internet connection, a few good pictures, and the willingness to open yourself up and put yourself out there. Though it may seem complicated, dating has never been this easy!

The increasing number of fantastic platforms available allow you to make endless first impressions, and come up with well thought-out responses without being put on the spot. Most importantly, they allow you to filter through thousands of profiles or potential matches and increase your chance of finding that perfect person. It is no longer a question of the right place and the right time, it's about the will and the right dating platform. While it might sound scary to be confronted with thousands of singles looking for love, the mechanisms of the dating sites and apps help you look for that needle in the haystack that is true love.

Dating websites and apps can be brilliant tools for finding your match. They provide you with ways to narrow down your search from the comfort of your own home, your office or on the go!

The first dating site was launched in 1995. Since then, much has changed since the introduction of the World Wide Web. With busy lives and steady friendship groups, many have turned to the world of the Internet to help them find the perfect match. Dating apps have become so popular that some even allow verified profiles for celebrities that wish to use them.

There are plenty of sites out there to suit everyone. From the big giants that match you using the latest technology, to app based sites like Tinder which are image based, to sites that revolve around interests and lifestyles from getting muddy in the country to specific interests in music. The world has woken up to the potentials of online dating and new users register on every platform every single day.

In 2015, Pew Research released statistics showing that 59% of Americans think that online dating is a good idea. Think about it: the population of the US is around 323 million, that could be you and millions of other people searching for love on the internet. There are many fish in the sea, and about half of them consider signing up for a dating site as a viable option.

Around 40 million Americans alone are using online dating sites and most dating coaches will advise you to at least give online dating a try. Sure, it's a change to go from traditional dating to online dating, but why not use all the means available to you. Many singles spend years looking for a relationship, so if you have the chance to improve your odds, it is definitely worth giving it a try.

Using an online dating site doesn't mean that you have to give up on traditional ways of dating. If anything, being on an online dating site will make you more open in real life to entertain the idea of going on a date.

Even the dating sites themselves are aware that online and traditional dating go hand-in-hand, and there is a trend for these sites to start organizing dating events such as speed dating in real-life.

There are over 1000 dating sites, and there is hardly a niche in society that does not have its own dating site yet. The top 3 dating services that are available at the moment are Match, eHarmony and Tinder. It makes sense to conduct some research before you choose the site that best suits your needs.

Match.com: Match is one of the original dating websites. It is still around and going strong and you can access it online or download the app. In fact, Match.com is so successful that it is now available in 24 countries and 15 different languages. It is based on a clever technology of algorithms that aims to pair you up with potential matches by calculating what is important to you and which characteristics you share. It's been matching people for over 20 years now, so it must be doing something right. Match.com has both free and paid versions of its app and site.

eHarmony: Like match.com you can use eHarmony online or download the app to your phone. And, just like the above eHarmony prides itself on its technology, so much so that they have patented the process! eHarmony pairs users based on common interests, as they believe that "opposites attract, then they attack." eHarmony will provide you with matched tailored to you, so think quality over quantity.

Tinder: Based on your Facebook account, Tinder has taken the world by storm with everyone working out whether to swipe left or right. Tinder is location based and mostly free. In comparison to Match.com and eHarmony it doesn't rely on an algorithm to show you potential matches. It will also take you much less time setting up your account, as all your information is already on your Facebook profile.

So, if you're ready to get started and find your perfect match, get reading and get dating!

Chapter 1 – How to Put Yourself Out There to Attract Your Match

Choosing the Right Dating Site

The internet is our one-stop shop for just about everything in the modern world, and dating is no different, Around 35-50% of couples owning up to having found love on the web. That is not to say that online dating doesn't still have a stigma attached to it. But don't pay too much attention to that. Most people who trash online dating are likely in relationships already or haven't yet mustered up the courage to open a profile themselves. Sure, it can be annoying to be shown an ex or your boss as a potential match, but you get over it. After all, you won't find anyone on a dating site who doesn't have a profile themselves, so they are in no position to judge.

This might be itching in your fingers already and you want to set up your profile. Slow down, because you will first want to figure out which site is the right match for you.

Since the population that uses dating sites has risen at such a quick rate, users have started to use sites that target a specific demographic with increasing frequency.

Be honest with yourself about what you're looking for and do some research before you dive in. You wouldn't buy the first car you see and you would look at more than one house before you move, so check out a few dating sites before you sign up.

If you're just looking to get over your fear of contact with dating sites you might want to opt for a site that doesn't take long to set up. If you've had it with not meeting a viable partner in real life and want to get going already, setting up a lengthy profile might feel worth the effort.

The first criteria many consider is whether a site is free or requires a membership plan. Some sites offer all their services for free, some require a monthly fee, others again use a freemium model. You might be able to look at potential matches for free, but you won't be able to send or receive messages. Some sites might not even give you the option to browse the other users before paying. As with any contract: be sure to read the fine print and terms and conditions before signing up.

If you decide that you are serious about looking for love on a specific dating site then by all means, invest a little money and buy that subscription. You don't have to go for the most expensive site from the get go, and if it's too flashy you might want to stay away from it for now. Add the cost to the money you spent on your a new outfit for your first dates and consider it all an investment in love. You will increase your chances not only because you are taking the endeavour seriously, but because your potential matches will immediately consider you more seriously. You are not alone. Whoever you send that first message to will have paid for the same position as you.

Don't pay for every feature offered, though. You're only just starting out and you don't want to spend all your money on the dating sites that might not even be the best option for you.

Sites that rely on algorithms will pair you up according to many factors.
These can be search criteria that you've decided are important to you. Say you are looking for a non-smoker, with an athletic build and an interest in literature, for example. Many sites will give you options to filter your searches so that you end up with more results that are "your type".

On most of those sites, you will be asked to answer hundreds of questions - don't worry, not all of them are mandatory - and the algorithm will match people that all chose flying as their superpower of choice.

These sites also record your behavior and see what kind of profiles you are attracted to. Location-based sites often contain much less information. Apps like Tinder or Happn show users to you that are or have been a certain distance from your current location. You won't have much to go on other than first impressions from pictures and brief profiles, so these apps still have the stigma attached of being superficial or for hookups only. Don't be discouraged, behavior varies according to location and age group and many couples have fallen in love through these apps.

Feel free to browse a few of the sites out there. You might want to sign up for a paid site that relies on algorithms, have a profile on a site that caters to your particular interest, and have a game-like app like Tinder or Happn at the same time. When looking for a partner in real life you don't stick to one particular coffee shop as your "hunting ground" because you consider it unfair to the coffee shop and its customers if you frequent another bar as well.

Most of the sites will offer you a free version or a trial membership, so give them a spin. If it works for you or you see someone interesting, subscribe. If you realize that that horticultural dating site doesn't really fit you, move on to the next site.

Unless you have signed up to niche dating sites that contradict one another you will see the same person on multiple sites. And they will see you. That's good, you're putting yourself out there!

Creating Your Profile

If you are anything like me, the idea of writing your resume fills you with dread, and the profile page of a dating site has just the same effect on you. You may be like my friend who loves nothing more than filling out questionnaires and personality tests. Whatever your feelings about answering personal questions, on most sites you can't get around it.

Rules about your username will vary depending on the dating app. While Tinder theoretically requires you to use your real name, other sites will require for you to come up with a username. Balance is key. Choose something witty, but don't choose something that only another die hard fan of an obscure foreign movie will understand. Try to choose a username that conveys what you are looking for. If your username starts with something "sexy...", most potential matches may not see you as someone who is looking for a serious relationship.

However, don't be scared! There is no time limit for filling in your profile and you can always go back and add more details or take out information.

You want to introduce yourself to a potential match, so you need that profile. It will be the first thing they see about you, and if it doesn't capture their attention it could be the last. Use the curiosity gap to your advantage. Intrigue your potential matches, but be just vague enough to make them curious for more.

Whatever you do, be honest! You don't have to be honest to a fault, no one is and no one expects you to list your entire list of guilty pleasures. But consider this - in life and online dating - treat others as you want them to treat you. Don't lie about your age, your profession or your marital status. You can maybe embellish that you are a bigger jazz fan than you are, but don't claim you're an expert skydiver if you're not. Remember, the goal is to meet your matches for a date. Meeting at a jazz bar will be okay, but you don't want to find yourself on a date expected to jump out of a plane when really you are terrified of heights.

Consult your friends before you write your profile. Many of them will have experience with online dating themselves. They might also be more objective than you when it comes to listing your strengths. Have a look at your social media accounts, too. Not only will your future matches be checking you out as well, so this might be the ideal time to delete those pictures of you and your ex. But chances are you will see what you've been up to recently, and you can add details to your profile.

When you start writing about yourself, keep it short. Attention spans aren't what they used to be and you're just trying to introduce yourself, not writing an autobiography. On the other hand, don't use one-word answers. You don't want to come off as too aloof or too cool for everything.

Keep in mind who your audience is. This is not a job application, so start with listing some of your interests. There's no need to include your employment history, you don't want to tell people too much about yourself already. Leave some information for the first conversation or date.

If possible, try to focus on positive things. If you are currently battling depression, there are special dating platforms just for you. Some general dating services however might even decline your profile. You're taking positive steps to improve your love life, so even if your life is messy at the moment, you're on your way to better times.

Provide some information that can be used as a conversation starter. Mention a good book you are reading or an upcoming vacation. Just remember to keep it relevant and revisit your profile frequently to update it for your suitors! If you still claim to be reading the same book a year later, people might start to wonder what's going on.

Don't be afraid to include specific interests or fears. Your match might like cats, too. If you hate spiders, you don't want a potential match with a pet tarantula to focus on you. Small details can prove very helpful to weed out matches or to catch people's interest.

Unfortunately, gender bias exists in the world of online dating as well. For example, surveys have shown that men that include the words "divorce", "ex" or "children" get more responses than average, whereas women get fewer. That doesn't mean you should lie or hide your history, everyone has baggage, just be aware that discrepancies exist and adjust accordingly.

Choosing Profile Photos

Choosing your profile picture can seem like a horrendous task. The same rules apply: be honest.

Find a picture that represents who you are. You would preferably use a picture on which you are smiling, but if that feels fake, don't. If you don't have any pictures you like, ask your friends for help. Resist the temptation to post a professional picture, you could be taken for a bait profile. On the other hand, choose a picture where you can actually be seen. Don't crop out half of your face, or hide behind sunglasses or a blurry photo resolution. Your potential matches might think that you have something to hide or that you're not serious about finding a match.

Studies show that profiles that include a close up and a full body shot do best. You want your match to be interested in you, so post a picture that you like, but make it a recent one. If your appearance has changed recently, don't worry. Make sure it reflects in your picture, you don't want your match to leave your first date feeling duped. No one expects you to look like a Hollywood star, so resist that temptation to photoshop your picture. You don't need it, and people have different tastes. You are looking for a partner in real life, the photoshop lie will only bring you so far. Creating your profile gives you a chance to have a fresh start.

A group shot might show that you are social and know how to have fun, but you don't want your matches to have to search for you or mistake you for someone else in the photo. You are trying to find a date for yourself!

A picture can contain lots of information, so try to choose an expressive one. It's advisable that you have at least one picture that shows one of your interests, whether it's skiing or your dog. If you're a parent and want to include your child, that's okay, but stay away from pictures including children if you do not have any. You could keep away potential matches if they assume the child is yours, and that is not the goal you are trying to achieve.

If you're still not sure which picture to choose, try looking at some examples of successful dating profiles. Dating sites want their users to find matches, as this is how their reputation grows. Major dating sites like eHarmony and Match have started publishing surveys that help users determine which profiles do well. Don't even think about posting that photo you took with your phone in a mirror, most users describe it as a turn off. But trends change all the time, so try to stay on top of things.

Keep taking the time to tweak and add to your information, and before you know it you will have a complete profile. Don't procrastinate. Put up your profile and start searching!

If you're not convinced yet or still feel too shy to write your own profile, don't despair. You can have all the fun of online dating without having to worry about how to sell yourself or what to highlight about your character. Chances are you will ask your friends for advice on how to brave the new world of online dating, so you could also ask them to help you set up a profile. Sites like mysinglefriend.com let your friends describe you and look for matches for you.

Make sure to pick a friend you trust and who knows your taste in partners. Dating profiles set up by friends can be a lot more snarky than you envisioned.

If you've heard too many horror stories about meeting with people found online and are not yet willing to meet complete strangers, give dating sites like Coffee Meets Bagel a chance. This app will only introduce you to singles that are friends of your Facebook friends. Having mutual friends provides the added benefit that you immediately have conversation topics.

Chapter 2 – How to Pick the Right Match

The first few hours and even days on a dating site can be frustrating. Remember, you're new and not a lot of people will even have had the chance to see your profile. So if you don't immediately get loads of requests and messages, don't take it personally. Take this time to keep updating and improving your profile, and think about what you are looking for in a match.

Naturally, everyone would love to find a good looking, successful and romantic partner. You're not new to this world, you know that beauty fades, wealth can be lost and a good job doesn't necessarily vouch for a good character. Think about characteristics of a future partner that are less obvious but leagues more important. Sharing the same interests or the same sense of humor are always good places to start, and you will figure out what interests you quickly.

This could be an opportunity to rethink your love life choices so far and get out there and meet some new people. You're looking for a partner because your choices so far didn't work out. Think about patterns in your past relationships and consider if they are contributing to the problem.

Make a list of the qualities that you look for in a partner but keep your list reasonable. Don't automatically disregard a potential match because he doesn't have a postgraduate degree or plays football professionally. Don't judge a book by its cover. There's more to you than you could fit into your profile, and there certainly is more to your potential matches as well.

Think about the following and write down what you are looking for in regards to each option:

-Looks
-Career
-Hobbies/interests
-Emotions
-What you want from a relationship/what they want from a relationship
-Pet peeves

See that list? You might have considered looks to be the most important factor, but finding a match with your favorite eye-color won't help bridge the gap if one of you is looking for something serious and the other is just looking to have fun.

You most definitely have thought about these points before, but by noting it down you make it easier to decide whether they are make-or-break qualities. Be aware that many of the algorithms used by dating sites will factor your decisions into their formula. If you click on a lot of blonde profiles, more profiles of this kind will appear in your feed.

Online dating offers you the chance to date people that you normally wouldn't meet. There are so many people on these sites and they come from all walks of life. Naturally, not all of them frequent the same places you do. These platforms allow you to meet people you may have never considered before.

Don't be too harsh about pictures. Suddenly we all wake up and have more wrinkles or less toned muscles than we used to have. Extend the same courtesy you want extended towards you and don't decide based on superficial reasons alone.

Online dating allows you a great opportunity to meet new and interesting people in a relatively safe environment. You don't have the distractions of a bar or sports event, but you run the risk to behave like a child in a candy store. Take the chance to move out of your comfort zone and talk to matches that have different interests than you. It's completely appropriate to talk to several people at once. But don't overwhelm yourself. The large number of potential matches might make you numb. Tinder alone has 1.6 billion swipes a day, you don't want your approach to be too casual. You should enjoy every Tinder match you get, but don't forget you are one of 26 billion matches made worldwide.

Ultimately, it is up to you how you would like to find a match. You might prefer quantity over quality or the other way around. There are multiple strategies to find your perfect match. While your choice of dating site will already put a few constraints on possible matches, your strategy will do the rest.

You might opt for a small search radius and a rather large amount of criteria that leave you with a small but exquisite batch of potential matches.

Or you might decide that you're going to dive head on in. Some people opt to talk to every match they receive, so as not to rule out potential partners based on superficial reasons. You don't have to find your strategy on day one. Most likely you will be too overwhelmed to know what works for you anyway.

Getting What You Want From an Online Chat

Even though you haven't met in a bar or in person, this part of the online dating experience is just the same as the conversation you would have if you bumped into each other in the outside world. Someone has to make the first step and the first line should be intriguing enough to keep the conversation going. The fact is, you are not their only match made today, so make it an individual approach that your match will remember.

Whilst online dating allows you to date in your pajamas and talk to people from the safety and comfort of your own home, you need to follow the normal rules of conversation.

Language

You are trying to get to know someone, and for now writing is your only way of connecting with them. Use proper English and complete sentences. Emojis are subjective, but you don't want to overdo it.

Once again, write a message the way you would want to receive one. Don't copy and paste a cheap or sleazy pick up line. Unless you are using a site that is specifically and explicitly geared towards sex and towards sex alone, do not use sexual innuendos or comments on their physical attributes to start the conversation. It comes off to most as tasteless, and most people who are serious about these sites will not tolerate that.

If you can, reference something found on your match's profile. Music or vacations can be good openers. Think of the details you included in your profile to attract attention. There's a reason you wrote about your favorite movies, so there's a reason your match has included favorite past times as well.

Be You- Be Nice

Online dating is a great way to meet people, and if you started chatting to a potential match there must have been a reason. Whether it is because of the algorithm or because the two of you decided that you simply like the way the other person looks or what's on their profile. Remember to relax, be yourself and be nice. The first chat provides a great way to find out more about your match and to ask the questions that are important to you. However, this is not an interview or an inquisition, take it in turn asking questions and make sure you really read the replies. The conversation should flow, so don't just rattle down a list of prepared questions.

Keep things friendly and try and stay away from awkward or contentious subjects if they aren't on your make or break list. Think about it twice before you write a joke or a sarcastic comment. You don't know each other yet and on paper jokes can be a lot less funny. If your humor matches, great. Remember, there are no rules cut into stone that you need to adhere to in order to chat with someone.

Be Assertive

Confidence is a very attractive quality. Don't sell yourself short. Don't be afraid to answer questions truthfully for fear of offending, be confident in your answers and show your match what a great person you are. Equally, don't be afraid to ask questions. If you get the impression that someone is looking for something more or less serious than you are, feel free to address it. Better to find out early than to go on a date that is doomed to end in disappointment.

It's the 21st century. Women, you are most certainly allowed to make that first advance towards a man. Besides, many people appreciate when a woman is confident enough to make a move first. You are both on a dating site, the intentions are clear from the get go.

Use Common Sense

While the online dating system provides great opportunities for meeting people, it's important to remember and realize that not everybody has the same intentions. If you are talking to a new match, don't be afraid to go with your gut feeling. There are dating sites specifically for sexual relationships, but that doesn't mean you won't find people looking solely for those on a site for romantic relationships. If you're unsure, state your intentions clearly or ask. If you are uncomfortable with the direction a chat is going, say goodbye. Don't feel guilty about it, not every match will work out.

The joy of online dating is that you can end a conversation and move on without lengthy dates and awkward silences. As with any new skill, practice makes perfect. There is nothing wrong with talking to a few frogs and learning who to avoid, it allows you to filter down the potential matches and helps increase the chances of you meeting face to face with someone that you really like and get on well with.

While the chances are low, there is always the risk of online predators. Don't give out personal information to your match. You wouldn't give all your details to a first date in real life, so the same rules apply here.

If you feel very insecure about handing out personal information you can choose a dating site that has a built in phone app. That way you can get to know your match better before handing out your phone number.

If you feel harassed by someone or expect them to be a fake profile, report them or block them. There will always be a few bad apples, that doesn't mean you need to buy them. Reporting a profile that doesn't use the site as it is intended is also a way of paying it forward. You might have noticed the apple is rotten, someone else might not. This is not you being vindictive, it is you looking out for your fellow singles.

Top Tips for the First Message You Send:

Read the profile of the person you are contacting carefully. Pick out information to refer to and show that you've taken the time to read it.

Don't start your message with a plain "hello". It's a polite greeting, but it's not very interesting. Chances are your match has received identical messages already. Instead, go with an interesting subject line or an icebreaker to make you stand out.

Leave the ball in their court. Include a couple of questions or an invitation to get back in touch with you.

Don't overdo it. Your match will be able to tell if you use the same enthusiastic compliment in every message. Though you may be excited to find someone that truly interests you, you don't want to scare them off! Give them time to become excited about you!

Chapter 3 – How to Move On and Arrange a Meet-up

Congratulations, you have your first matches and the conversation is going smoothly. If you've been talking and it's going well, it's time to think about taking it to the next level, and arranging a meeting. Remember, the person isn't real until you meet them.

You might start this process by exchanging phone numbers first. Maybe there is no chemistry at all when you talk on the phone, you won't know until you try. It has become common to exchange social media profiles too. You might not want to continue the conversation on the dating site, if only for the sole reason that you are paranoid that your match is simultaneously looking for other matches.

If you aren't quite sure, or you are feeling nervous, suggest a chat on the phone, or even better- a video chat! It can be nice to put a voice to the face and name and it can make it feel a little bit more like a 'normal' date. Not everyone is equally charming in writing as on the phone and vice versa.
Alternatively, a video chat would give the both of you an opportunity to speak directly to each other before meeting in person.

Theoretically, there is no time limit for when you should be getting to this point, but remember that life continues outside of the bubble that is the dating platform.
Studies have shown that dates are more likely to be successful if they happen between 17 and 23 days

of initial contact. After that, you might have built your match up so much in your head that the date ends up disappointing expectations. There is also always the risk that one of you will find another, more interesting match.

Don't fret if you don't hear from your match for a while. While online dating can be time consuming, people have a life outside of the dating sites. Not getting an immediate reply doesn't automatically mean your match has lost interest, it could just be that their work meeting that is going longer, or aren't in a position to access their messages at that time. Keep calm and wait things out. Of course, be reasonable with yourself! If its been a week and you still have not heard back from them, consider it time to move on. This move when someone decides to stop communicating without warning is known as "ghosting", and is an unfortunate occurrence.

Once you've exchanged the first few messages, you should have an idea if you'd like to meet your potential match. Trust yourself. If you are endlessly exchanging messages and you still don't feel the spark, then save yourself the stress and move on. You don't have to go on dates just because you are paying for the service, or just because the other person insists!

If you like the person that you are talking to, be brave and ask if they would like to meet. Remember, confidence makes you attractive. If they say yes, fantastic. You can start planning your date.

If they say no, that's alright too. It is not about you, so don't take it personal. Your match only knows what little information is on your profile, so don't take a no as a rejection of your character. Even experienced online daters have to continuously test the waters and work on opening themselves up to new things, just as what you have done!

Respect their decision if your match declines a date. They might just think it's too soon, they might be busy, or they might just not be into you. If the conversation ends at this point then move on. If it continues then give them a chance to ask you out, but don't waste your time. You should be able to tell if they are working towards asking you out, or if they're just being by trying to keep in touch with you.

Once you've set the date, keep in contact; let your match know that you are looking forward to meeting them, keep the conversation light and positive, as this will help you remain confortable with the idea of eventually meeting them.

If for some reason you can't make the date or change your mind, be honest with your match and tell them as soon as possible. As with everything, honesty is the best policy, whether you've been on another great date with someone else, or the spark isn't quite there with this person. You would respect and expect the same courtesy.

Chapter 4 – Best Places to Meet-Up

When planning the first date, less is more!

Remember that you haven't yet met this person. And even though you think the two of you get on fantastically online, you never really know what the chemistry is going to be like face-to-face.

Depending on the dating site, the first date can be extremely short. It is not uncommon, for example, for Tinder dates to decide within seconds of meeting that there is no chemistry. It's part of the game, even if it seems cruel.

The more honest you have been on your profile and when getting to know one another online, the more likely it will be that your date will be enjoyable. It is unlikely that you will meet the love of your life on your very first date, but you will meet some interesting people and hopefully experience a few fun evenings.

Though more and more dating sites have started to include background checks, you don't know who you are meeting. Don't immediately invite your date to your home. Not only does it convey the wrong message from the start, it also puts you at risk unnecessarily.

Always go for a place that is comfortable and relaxed. Picking a nice bar is a great choice as you will be surrounded by people and in a relaxed atmosphere. You can try to go for a daytime coffee date as well, but pick a spot that spells date and not business meeting. Choose a place that has good traffic and is accessible to you. That way you will feel more comfortable if there are others are you, or decide to leave quickly if the date isn't working out.

If you are feeling confident that this is going to be a great date you should still play it safe. Pick a meeting point that is in public and somewhere close to other activities. You can always extend a date that was supposed to be a drink in a bar to a romantic dinner. There will always be fun activities to do. In winter, you can go ice skating if your chances of helplessly flailing around and falling are low, and if you feel confident whipping out your bathing suit on a first date you can always go for a swim in the summer.

While in planning mode, make sure that you think back to your conversations and consider what your match would be interested in. You probably already know enough about your match to plan a fun first date. If they mentioned that they don't drink, then taking them to a happy hour won't end in success. If you don't drink, now is your chance to mention that. The whole point of going on a first date is to have fun with one another and to get to know your match. Try to plan something that you both can enjoy and not something that caters specifically to your interests. And remember that nerves occur in everyone, so don't make it to overwhelming or too intimate.

It won't happen with every match but maybe the two of you have completely hit it off. If you are feeling confident and want to go for a more substantial date: go for something creative or quirky.

Great Ideas for a First Date:

Bowling – Bowling or something similar can be a great option if either of you have a competitive side. You might even discover that your competitive side matches perfectly. Bowling also gives you plenty of time to have a chat between strikes and to get to know each other better.

The Aquarium – If there's an aquarium in your city, it can be a fun and peaceful place for a date. It's a great activity in a calm and beautiful surrounding. You can test each other's fishy knowledge and learn a few new facts along the way. There's a reason the Aquarium is often used as a dating spot in romantic movies. You could also go to the zoo, though people have strong opinions about zoos, so you might want to check on that.

City tour – Whether you both live in the same city and want to share your secrets spots, or one of you made the trip for the date, a city tour can be a fun icebreaker and will provide you with lots of material for conversations. You can get out the map and plan your own tour or go with a preplanned option. Many cities now offer small independent tours designed to specific interests like street art or historical sites. When you've had enough you can stop at the first place that catches your interests and have a drink or a snack.

Comedy show – This is the ultimate icebreaker, providing opportunities to fall off your chair from laughing too much or gasping in horror with your date. Just don't sit to near the front or in the comedian's eye line, as you could become a target in their routine! Comedy shows can be tricky, so make sure first that you have a similar style of humor so neither of you leave offended or bored.

Live music – Find an open mic night or a performance by a local band. You can find a cozy spot to sit and will immediately be able to get chatting about music and the performances. Maybe one of you will even be inspired to grab the mic.

Go carting or to a fairground – This date has it all, but it can have its pitfalls. You don't want to spend your date vomiting because you couldn't stomach a ride, so pick this carefully. A first date that includes the fear factor can help attraction grow between you. Research shows that the adrenaline rush mimics the hormones of falling in love.

Any activity that fits both of your profiles – Don't go to a museum if it's your thing but not your matches'. But if by chance both of you are into indoor climbing, there's nothing better for a first date than that. Are you both dog lovers? Go to the park with your dogs; make it a double-date! The sky is the limit, especially if skydiving is your hobby of choice.

As online dating leads some singles to enter a frantic phase of 'shopping' for potential partners, but never actually meet them in person, there are a few dating sites that have changed the idea of online dating. Instead of putting the focus on the courtship phase of searching for profiles, liking, texting, exchanging numbers and coming up with an idea for a date, they put the focus on the date itself. Sites like howaboutwe.com shorten the time between the first contact and the first date. Users can suggest a date idea and if the idea appeals to other users they can join the date. You will have less time to figure out if you have chemistry or shared interest, but you will be going on fun dates that are unique and inventive.

If you had a bad date, go home and watch a feel good movie or talk it through with a friend. Bad dates are bound to happen. You will probably even have your share of awful experiences. Don't give up. As much as the dating sites are trying, dating and love aren't a science. You can be 100% compatible on paper yet there may not even be a hint of a spark.

Forget the awful dates and laugh about the bad ones. Remember to stay positive. You are putting yourself out there, you are making yourself vulnerable and you are doing the best you can. There's nothing more you can do, so be proud of yourself for trying, even in the face of failure.

Conclusion

Dating is always complicated, whether you tackle it in real life or brave the digital world of online dating.

Luckily, we have advanced far enough as a society that online dating has become a norm and not an exception. While online dating once carried the stigma that only "creeps" or desperate singles would sign up for dating site, it is now far less stigmatized. The majority of us have tried it or will try it one day. Even professional match makers no longer do their jobs without relying on social media, so why not do it yourself.

In any case, online dating means that you need to put yourself out there. When dating in real life, you have the advantage of being able to be aloof or ambiguous about your intentions. With online dating, the cards are on the table from the beginning. That can be intimidating, but it can also be freeing. You know that your potential matches have invested just as much time, if not more, as you did into building their profile and looking for love. You can meet people you would otherwise not have access to and you can weed through the masses based on information by your potential matches themselves. You no longer have to trust your aunt's words that her hairdresser's child is just perfect for you. You know that you and your match have at least one thing in common, even if it is only that you use the same dating site.

While it may feel awkward at first to approach someone virtually, it is no less awkward than walking up to a stranger and asking them for their number. You get a chance to talk to your match before you go on the first date, so you are unlikely to find yourself on a date with someone who is the complete opposite of what you are looking for. If you are using a location based dating app, you will likely soon start seeing people on the street whose profiles you have seen through your app! Obviously you shouldn't stalk them, but maybe their profile is worth revisiting once you realize that they shop at the same obscure record shop as you do. Or maybe you will finally have the guts to approach them. You know they are single and looking, this just gives you another chance to meet them.

Online dating doesn't promise immediate success, but it allows you to be open and honest with your match. You don't have to play games on your first date, pretending that you are looking for something far more casual than you are. In many cases, questions like whether you want to get married or have a family will already have been answered in the initial process. You can even choose a site that is specifically geared towards that audience.

For a long time during its initial phase, online dating wasn't very inclusive. Today, there are sites for anyone and everyone- you just have to take the time to research and figure out what you want to look for.

Dating sites are also taking into account that not every person who uses their services feel comfortable meeting a virtual stranger and are trying to make the process safer for everyone involved. Some sites offer background checks, so if you feel more comfortable with that you can still find a good site. Online dating doesn't grant you guaranteed security. Users should be aware that the internet will always be a place where people may hide their true intentions and character. But if you apply the same common sense you apply in real life you will steer clear from these pitfalls.

Remember that you are not the only one looking for love, so be fair when creating your profile and introducing yourself. Be open to meeting new people and to having a good time and in the best case you will be left with some hilarious stories, new friends, a compatible and loving partner, and the knowledge that you won't need your profile again.

The Three Most Important Rules to Online Dating Are Easy to Remember

Be honest! Be honest to yourself about what you are looking for and be honest to your potential matches. Lies you tell on your profile or pictures that don't represent the real you will come back to haunt you. The longer the lie lasts, the longer you will have to play a part that is not you, and the longer it will take for you to instill your own self-confidence.

Treat others the way you want to be treated. Don't just match other singles only to never initiate contact or to ignore their messages. Be polite. If a conversation is getting out of hand, trust yourself and leave. Otherwise, find it in your heart to be kind enough to explain that this match won't work out and say goodbye. Don't stand up your dates. Don't treat people as sexual objects. If you are serious about online dating, find someone who is just as serious.

Don't despair. No one should be forcing you into online dating. If you're absolutely sure that it's not for you, then let it be. But don't let every match that didn't work out or every bad date tempt you into deleting your profile. Every Jack has his Jill. Maybe they are just not online yet.

If you follow these rules, you are good to go! You will have exciting times, fun times, boring lulls, sizzling chemistry, and maybe even bad dates. Maybe your foray into online dating will lead to marriage, or maybe your aunt's neighbor was the right match all along. You won't know until you try something new.

Printed in Poland
by Amazon Fulfillment
Poland Sp. z o.o., Wrocław